FRED
GETS
DRESSED

PETER BROWN

Fred is naked.

He romps through the house

naked and wild and free.

He romps around his bedroom

and across the hall

and into Mum and Dad's bedroom.

Fred might never get dressed!

But what's this? Fred has stopped romping.

He peeks into Mum and Dad's wardrobe.

He walks through the door.

Fred looks at Dad's side of the wardrobe.

He thinks about the way Dad dresses.

It might be fun to dress like Dad.
So Fred carefully picks out a shirt
and a tie and a pair of shoes.

But he has trouble putting them on.

Fred looks at Mum's side of the wardrobe.

He thinks about the way Mum dresses.

It might be fun to dress like Mum.
So Fred carefully picks out a blouse
and a scarf and a pair of shoes.

He has no trouble putting them on,
but he is not finished yet.

He walks out of the wardrobe
and over to Mum's table.

The shoes he's wearing are big
and wobbly, so he has to go slow.

Fred picks through Mum's
jewellery box and make-up drawer.

He thinks about Mum's different styles.

Fred knows what to do with jewellery.

But what are these things for?

Before Fred can clean his face,
Mum and Dad come stomping into the room.

Mum picks out
different cases and
tubes and brushes.

She begins doing her make-up and her hair.

Fred watches closely and follows along.

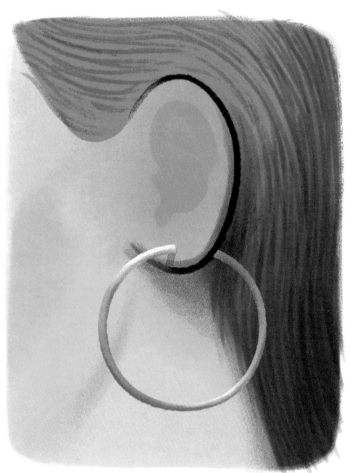

The whole family

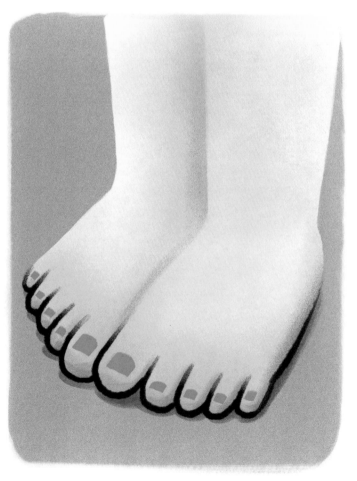

joins the fun.

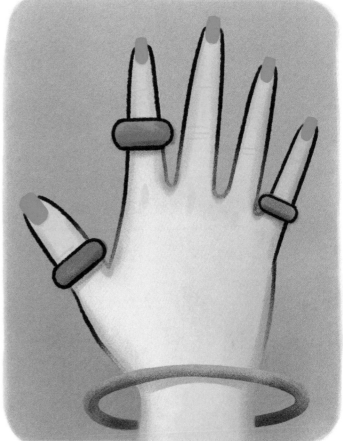

Now Fred is dressed.

Well, mostly dressed.